Clever Joe

☆ **3** Watch the story. 5 Listen and read.

1 I'm in class 3a

☆ **1** **Work in pairs. How many words can you remember?**

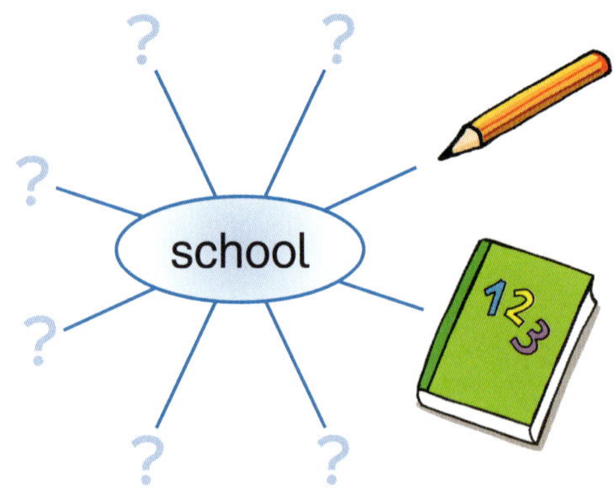

We can remember … words.

☆☆ **2** **How many of the words can you read?**

pen	pencil	pencil case	rubber	ruler	scissors
book	glue stick	chair	schoolbag	desk	

☆ **3** 1 6 **Listen and point. Then test your partner.**

1 German
2 English
3 Maths
4 Art
5 Music
6 PE

☆☆ **4** **Work in pairs. Ask and answer.**

Do you like PE?

What's your favourite subject?

Yes, I do. / No, I don't.

English.

Poster 1 AB S. 4 + KV 2

Gerngross · Puchta · Becker

PLAYWAY 3

PUPIL'S BOOK

Starter
School is cool 2

Unit 1
I'm in class 3a 4

Unit 2
At the pet shop 10

Unit 3
The spooky castle 16

Unit 4
My family 22

Unit 5
Clothes 28

Unit 6
Birthdays.............................. 34

Unit 7
It's lunch time! 40

Unit 8
My day 46

Unit 9
Body 52

Special days

Thanksgiving 58

Christmas 59

Easter 61

School is cool

☆ **1** 1–2 **Listen and point. Sing the song. Test your partner.**

Oh, what a lovely morning

You're in bed,
and you wake up.
You check your watch.
It's time to get up!

Oh, what a lovely morning,
it's time to go to school.
Oh, what a lovely morning,
school is so cool!

Wash your face,
put on your clothes.
Have a glass of milk.
Take your bag and off you go!

Oh, what a lovely morning,
it's time to go to school.
Oh, what a lovely morning,
school is so cool!

☆☆ **2** 4 **Listen and read. Then change the dialogue and act it out.**

Grace: Harry?
Harry: Yes, Grace?
Grace: I've got a new computer game.
Harry: Great.
Grace: Can you come to my house?
Harry: OK. When?
Grace: At three.
Harry: OK.
Grace: Great! Bye.
Harry: Bye.

AB S. 2

5 8 Listen and remember the numbers. Then say.

LOOK!
one glue stick – two glue sticks
one book – two books

6 Play the game.

LOOK!
There's one pencil.
(There's = There is)
There are three pencils.

KV 3 AB S. 5

★ 7 Listen and point.

I left my pullover in the gym.

Listen.

Draw a picture.

Take a pencil.

Colour.

May I go to the toilet?

Close your book.

Open your book.

I left my pencil case in the music room.

★★ 8 Work in pairs. Play a memory game.

AB S. 6

9 Read and answer.

I like Music.

I really don't like Art. I'm not very good at it.

My favourite subject is Maths. I'm good at it.

Naomi

I love Art. I'm good at it.

I don't like PE very much.

I don't like Music. I'm not very good at it.

Elliot

1. Music is cool. — Who's this?
2. PE? No, I don't like it. — Who's this?
3. I love Maths. — Who's this?
4. Music isn't for me. — Who's this?
5. Art really isn't my favourite subject. — Who's this?
6. My favourite subject is Art. — Who's this?

My text

10 Read. Write your own text.

My text

I'm in class 3b.

My schoolbag is cool. It's red and green.

I like English. I don't like German.

11 Read. Write your own text.

My text

I'm in class 3a this year. My favourite subject is Art. I'm good at it. I don't like Music. I'm not good at it.

I've got a very nice pencil case. In my pencil case, there's a pen, a ruler, a rubber, a glue stick and two pencils.

12 12–13 **Listen. Sing the song.**

My favourite subject

I like to run and jump,
I love to score a goal.
I like the sports we play.
We've got PE today.

PE is my favourite subject,
yeah, it's my number one!

Oh, really? Well …

I like the stories we read.
The songs are really cool.
I love the games we play.
Oh, we've got English today.

English is my favourite subject,
yeah, it's my number one!

Oh, really? Well …
German, Maths, English, Art or PE,
they're all so cool.
We love school!
… And Music too!
Yeah!

13 14 **Listen and read. Then change the dialogue and act it out.**

Boy: Do you like German?

Girl: Yes, it's my favourite subject. I'm good at it.
And what about you? What's your favourite subject?

Boy: It's PE. I love it.

Mia & Mike

A special guest

14 Look at the photos. Guess the answers. Watch the story and check.

- Who is Mia?
- Who is Mike?
- Who is the guest?
- Who is the teacher?

Number 1 is …

A group project: A guest in your class

Practise role plays in groups.

Hello, I'm …	Hello, I'm …
How are you?	I'm good. / OK. / Great. And you?
This is …	Nice to meet you.
This is my class / school. There are … girls and … boys.	
Look. This is my pencil / schoolbag / …	Cool. / Very nice.
Mrs / Mr …, this is (Paula) …	Hello, Mrs / Mr …

you / your friends

guest

At the pet shop

1 Work in pairs. How many words can you remember?

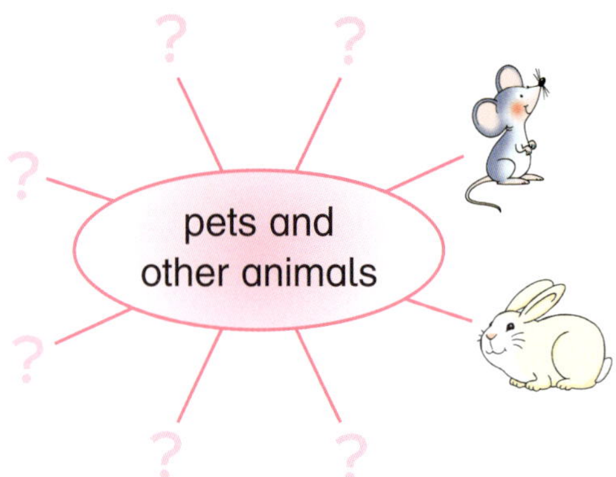

2 How many of the words can you read?

hamster	cat	fish	dog
rabbit	mouse	duck	rat

3 16 Listen and point. Then test your partner.

1. pony
2. snake
3. tortoise
4. spider
5. lizard
6. budgie
7. frog
8. guinea pig

4 Work in pairs. Ask and answer.

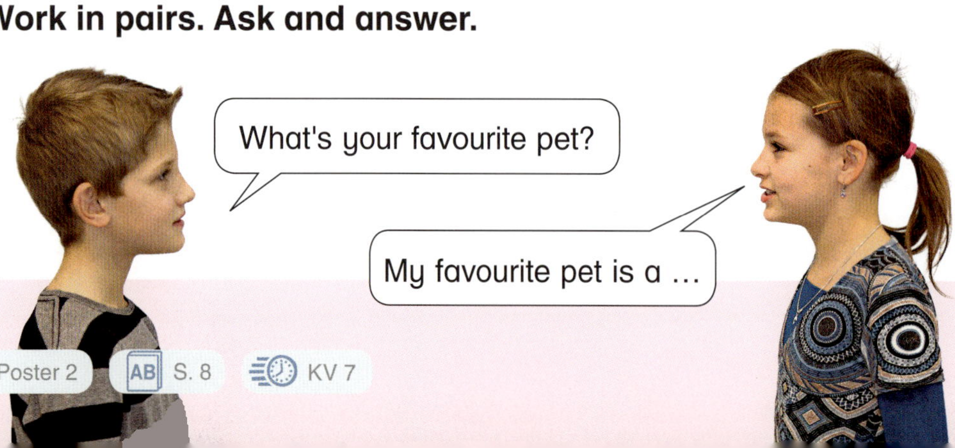

★ 5 Look and read.

★ 6 18 Listen and read.

★★ 7 Remember and speak.

☆ 8 20–21 **Listen. Sing the song.**

Mice, mice, mice

Mice, mice, mice,
I like their little ears.

Mice, mice, mice,
I like their little feet.

Mice, mice, mice,
I like their little teeth.
Yes, little mice are really nice!

My mum hates mice,
my dad hates mice,
but I think mice are really nice.

I give them cheese,
I give them rice.
Yes, mice are really nice!

☆ 9 Work with a partner. What animal is it?

1

2

3

4

5

6

7

8
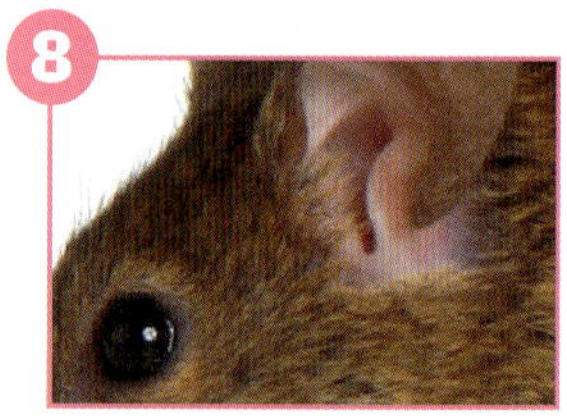

Pets

☆10 **Watch the story and say words you remember. Finish the sentences.**

☆☆11 22 **Listen and read.**

Tim: Where are you going, Sue?

Sue: To the pet shop.

Tim: Why?

Sue: I want to buy two rats.

Tim: Rats?

Sue: Yes, I like rats. They're very clever.

Tim: Can I come with you?

Sue: Yes, sure.

☆☆☆12 **Do a role play.**

13 Work in pairs. Ask and remember.

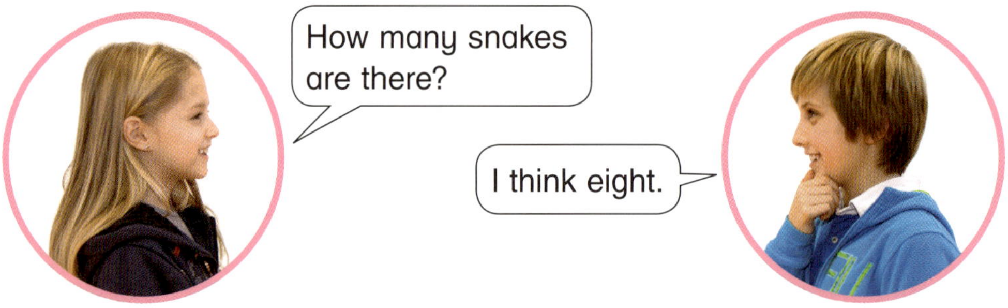

My text

14 Read. Write your own text.

My text

I haven't got a pet.
My grandma has got a budgie.
It's yellow and green.

15 Read. Write your own text.

My text

I've got a cat. My cat's name is Snuggles. He's white and grey and he has got black ears. I love Snuggles. He sleeps in my bed. Snuggles eats meat, fish and cheese. Yes, cheese! He loves cheese.

My sister has got a rabbit. Her name is Pepper. She eats carrots and broccoli. She doesn't like cheese.

Have you got a pet?

☆ 16 23 Listen and read.

☆☆ 17 Ask five classmates. Make notes.

Name	Animal	Colour	How old?
Natalie	hamster	brown	3 years
David	—	—	—

☆☆☆ 18 Tell the class.

3 The spooky castle

★ **1** 24 **Listen and point. Then test your partner.**

1 bats
2 spider's web
3 haunted forest
4 spiders
5 ghost
6 scary shadow
7 castle
8 mice
9 rats

★★ **2** **Work in groups. Play a chain game.**

3 Look at the picture on page 16. Can you answer the questions?

1. How many spiders are there?
2. How many bats are there?
3. How many rats are there?
4. One spider likes oranges. What colour is it?
5. Two rats like chocolate. What colour are they?
6. Where's the big spider's web?
7. Where's the scary shadow?
8. What's the big ghost's name?
9. What's the small ghost's name?
10. Where's the chocolate?
11. Where's the haunted forest?
12. What colour is Edwin's bed?

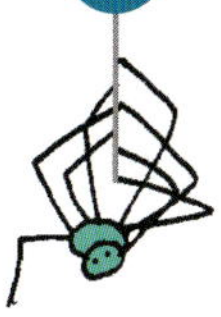

4 How many true sentences can you make? How many untrue sentences can you make?

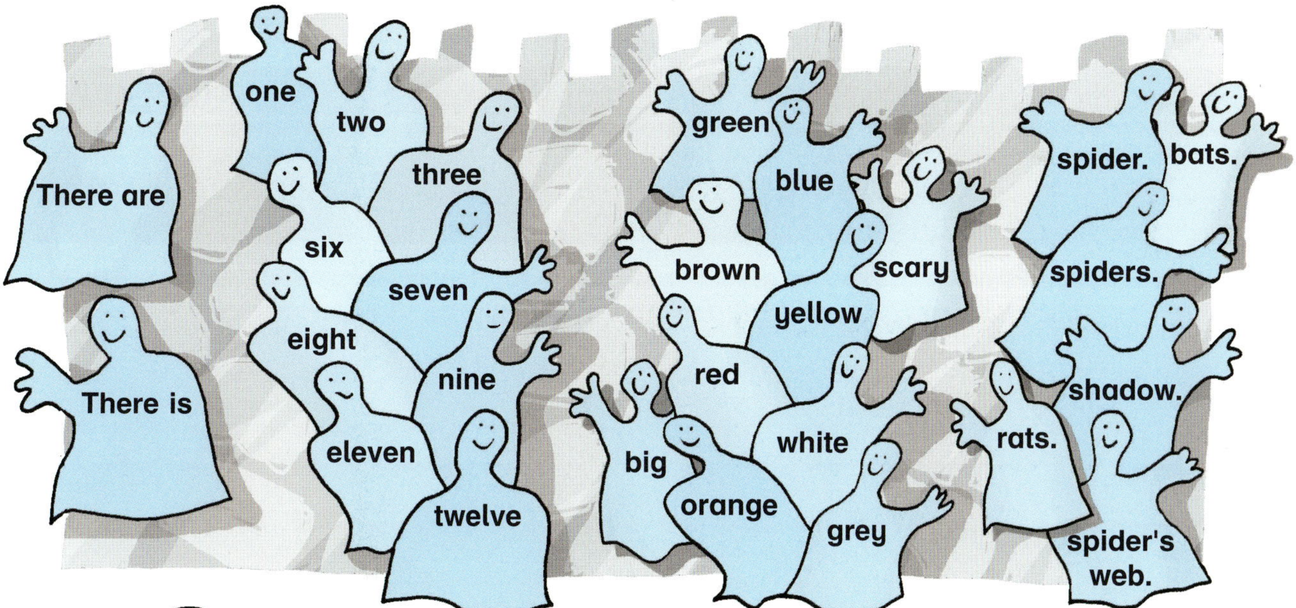

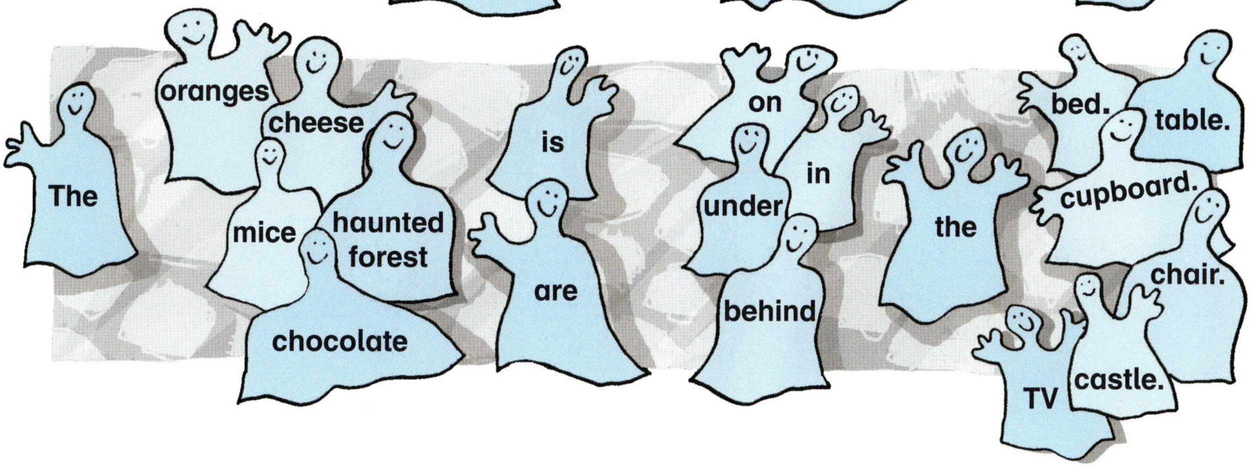

I'm scared

5 **Watch the story and say words you remember. Finish the sentences.**

6 26 **Listen and read.**

Ryan: Help!

Lucy: What is it, Ryan?

Ryan: I'm scared.
There's a monster in my bed.

Lucy: Come on, let's check. …
Here's your monster. Raaah!

Ryan: Lucy! I'll get you!

Lucy: Good night!

7 **Do a role play.**

8 27–28 Listen. Sing the song.

The spooky castle

In the middle of the wood
there's a castle dark and old,
dark and old.

There are spiders,
there are rats,
there are owls
and there are bats
in the spooky, spooky castle
in the middle of the night.

When the clock strikes twelve,
the ghosts begin to sing:
hoo hooah hoo.

There are spiders,
there are rats, …

When the clock strikes twelve,
the ghosts begin to dance:
hoo hooah hoo.

Hooah hooah hooah hoo,
hooah hooah hooah hoo
in the spooky, spooky castle
in the middle of the night.

When the clock strikes twelve,
oh yeah, they sing and dance:
hoo hooah hoo.

9 Draw and speak.

In our spooky castle there are five spiders.

There are three ghosts. On the bed there's a lion. His name is Rocky.

AB S. 16

10 29 **Listen and read. Find the photographs.**

Castles in Scotland

Every summer, thousands of tourists come to Scotland. Many of them want to see the beautiful castles. One of them is Edinburgh Castle.

There are lots of lakes in Scotland. The Scottish word for lake is 'loch'. Loch Ness is a famous lake.

Some people say there's a monster in that lake. The monster is called Nessie. Is Nessie a fish? A dinosaur? Nobody knows.

Urquhart Castle is on Loch Ness. It's one of the oldest and biggest castles in Scotland. It's more than 800 years old.

1

2

3

4

I'm not scared

11 30 **Listen and point.**

bear

truck

goat

house

log

mat

boat

fly

12 31 **Listen and say the poem.**

I'm not scared

I'm not scared of
a croc in my sock,
a bee on my knee,
or a bird in my shirt,
but I am scared of
a fly in my eye.

13 **Write your own poem and draw a picture.**

a goat on my boat

a rat on my hat

a bear on my chair

a mouse in my house

a bat on my mat

a snake in my cake

a duck in my truck

a frog on a log

4 My family

☆ 1 Work in pairs. How many words can you remember?

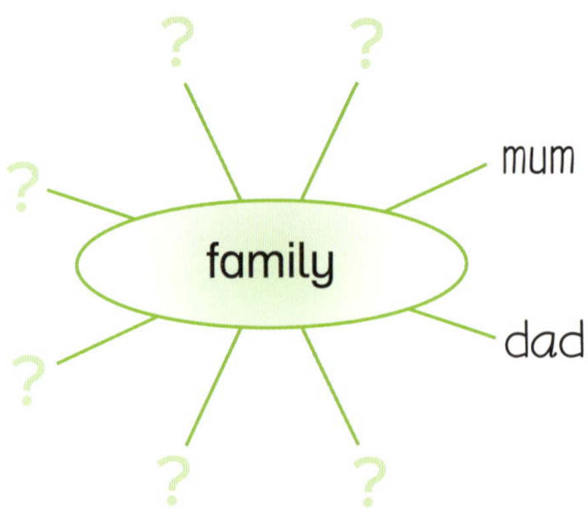

☆☆ 2 How many of the words can you read?

brother	sister	mum	dad
aunt	uncle	grandpa	grandma

☆ 3 2/1 Listen and point. Then test your partner.

1. clever
2. friendly
3. fit
4. musical
5. funny

☆☆ 4 Work in pairs. Play a memory game.

★ **5** Work in pairs. Say.

Katie

Sam

Ruby

Oscar

Poppy

Jamie

Elsa

Liam

Alyssa

Felix

What about Liam?

He's very fit.

★ **6** 2 3–4 Listen. Sing the song.

Emma's family

Emma's brother Henry
is clever and so friendly.
Emma's sister Abigail
is funny and so musical.

Emma, Henry, Abigail
are my best friends.
We have lots of fun
at school and at weekends.

Emma's brother Henry
plays basketball and swims.
Emma's sister Abigail
is musical and sings.

A present for Joe

☆ **7** **Watch the story.** 2 6 **Listen and read.**

Bella?
Ask Bella.
Yes, my sister.
Oh, do you like it? Your brother doesn't want to play with me.
That's a great football, Joe.
Really? I love your football. But I can't play with you. I'm going swimming. Bye.
Bye, Bella.
Oh!
Aaarrrrggghhh! This football is stupid, Dad.
It's not fair. My friends don't want to play with me. Aaaarrrggghhh!
Yes, my son?
Dad?
Dad. I'm really sorry. The football isn't stupid. I was angry.
That's OK, Joe.
And now let's go and play football, OK?
Thanks, Dad.
Yes, Dad.
Just a minute, Joe.
Oh, hello. This is Joe's Dad. I've got an idea...
Oh, hello everyone. What a nice surprise. Come and play football with us.
Yes. Let's play football. Great idea.
Wow. Really?
Well done, Joe!
Good shot, Joe.

8 2/7 **Listen and read.**

Interviewer: Excuse me. My name is Zara, I'm a reporter with the school magazine. Can I ask you some questions?

Boy: No problem.

Interviewer: Tell me about yourself.

Boy: My name is Riley. I'm in class 3c. I live in Leeds.

Interviewer: How old are you, Riley?

Boy: I'm nine.

Interviewer: What about your family?

Boy: Well, there's my mum and dad and I've got a brother and a sister.

Interviewer: How old are they?

Boy: My sister is seven and my brother is five.

Interviewer: And who's your best friend?

Boy: Adam. He's in my class.

Interviewer: What's your favourite subject?

Boy: English. I love it.

Interviewer: Thanks so much.

Boy: That's OK. Bye.

Interviewer: Bye.

9 Change the dialogue in 8 and act it out.

My text

10 Read. Write your own text.

My text

This is my family.
My mum, my two sisters and me, and our dog, Blackie. Blackie is very clever.

11 Read. Write your own text.

My text

My name is Quinn. I'm eight years old. I've got a brother and a sister. Ryan, my brother, is ten. And Kirsty, my sister, is eleven. They're great. Ryan is very musical and he's in a band. And Kirsty is clever. Her favourite subject is Maths.

Families

12 Look at the photos. Guess the answers. Then watch the video and check.

1 

2 

3 

4 

5 

6 

Who's …

- Mia's mum?
- Mia's dad?
- Mia's sister?
- Mike's mum?
- Mike's brother?
- Mike's sister?

A project: Introduce your family

Bring photos or draw pictures of your family. Introduce your family.

This is my mum / dad.
This is my sister / brother (Jenny / Bob).
He's / She's … (years old).
This is my …

Presentation tip:

- ✔ Loud and clear!
- ✔ Smile.
- ✔ Point at your picture / photo.

5 Clothes

☆ **1 Work in pairs. How many words can you remember?**

☆☆ **2 How many of the words can you read?**

woolly hat	pullover	jeans	trainers	T-shirt
cap	jacket	skirt	socks	shoes

☆ **3** 2 9 **Listen and point. Then test your partner.**

1. mittens
2. trousers
3. scarf
4. tights
5. hoodie
6. boots
7. slippers

☆☆ **4 Play the game.**

★ 5 ② 11–13 Listen. Do the chant.

Cold and hot

It's cold outside.
Put on your jacket.
It's cold outside.
Put on your hat.
It's cold outside.
Put on your mittens.
OK, let's go.

Let's go inside.
OK, let's go.
It's hot in here.
Take off your mittens.
It's hot in here.
Take off your hat.
It's hot in here.
Take off your jacket.
Ah, that's better.

★★ 6 Play the guessing game.

The hats in the attic

★ **7** Watch the story. 2/16 Listen and read.

☆ 8 Match and say.

blue trainers with yellow stripes

orange trainers with a picture of a football

red and black trainers

white trainers with green stars

The red and black trainers are number … .

I think so too.

☆☆ 9 2/17 Listen and read. Then change the dialogue and act it out.

Matilda: Hello, Ms Butler.

Ms Butler: Hello, Matilda.

Matilda: I'm looking for my trainers.

Ms Butler: Just a moment. Are these your trainers?

Matilda: No, they're blue with white stripes.

Ms Butler: Ah, here they are.

Matilda: Thank you, Ms Butler.

☆ 10 Read the text. Find the correct picture.

She's wearing a yellow woolly hat. Her pullover is green, her skirt is red, her tights are blue and her trainers are white.

It's …

Lorraine | Sienna | Kim | Norah

☆☆ 11 Play a guessing game.

Her woolly hat is …

It's …

My text

☆☆ 12 Read. Write your own text.

My text

I like my green T-shirt, my black hoodie and my blue jeans.
I don't like my brown slippers.

☆☆☆ 13 Read. Write your own text.

My text

Here's a picture of Julia. She's my best friend. She's wearing a blue cap, a white scarf and a red pullover. Her red pullover is very nice. She's also wearing blue jeans and black boots. On her blue jeans there are red flowers.

Class survey

Favourite clothes

14 **Make a grid. In groups, ask and answer questions. Make notes.**

	T-shirt 1	T-shirt 2	T-shirt 3	T-shirt 4
Sophia	☺	☺	☺	☹
David	☹	☹	☺	☹
Lisa	☹	☺	☹	☺
Sam	☺	☹	☺	☹

15 **Write a group report. Then talk about your group.**

In our group, two children like T-shirt number 1.
Two children like T-shirt number 2.
Three children like T-shirt number 3.
Only one child likes T-shirt number 4.

6 Birthdays

LOOK!

My birthday**'s** in May. = My birthday **is** in May.

☆ **1** 2 20–22 **Listen. Do the chant.**

My birthday

My birthday's not in January,
in February or March.
My birthday's not in April,
in May or in June.

It isn't in July, in August
or September.

It isn't in October
or even in November.

Remember, remember,
my birthday's in December.

☆☆ **2** 2 23 **Listen. Then test your partner.**

Winter.

December, …

☆☆ **3** 2 24 **Listen. Then play a guessing game.**

Sandra, is your birthday in summer?

No, it isn't.

Is it in autumn?

Yes, it is.

Is it in September?

No, it isn't.

Is it in October?

Yes, it is.

Daisy's birthday

4 **Watch the story and say words you remember. Finish the sentences.**

5 25 **Listen and read. Do a role play.**

Olivia: I wish you a happy birthday, Rose.

Rose: Thank you, Olivia.

Alex: Happy birthday, Rose.

Rose: Thank you, Alex. Let's have some cake and orange juice.

Olivia: Great, thanks.

Rose: When's your birthday, Alex?

Alex: My birthday's in December.

Rose: And when's your birthday, Olivia?

Olivia: It's next week. On Friday. My party is on Sunday. Please come.

Alex & Olivia: Thanks, great.

★ **6** 2 28 **Listen and read. Match the invitations to the parties.**

1

Come to my party
on Saturday.

Bring your bike,
bring your ball,
and much more.
Come at four!

2

Come to my party on Sunday.

Are you scared of monsters?
Are you scared of rats?
Are you scared of snakes?
Or are you scared of bats?
See you then at two.
My house is near the zoo.

3

My party is on Friday.

Bring some oranges,
bring some kiwis,
bring bananas,
apples and pears.
Meet me at my door
right at four.

4

Please come to my party
on Saturday.

Meet me by the sea
at three.
Let's have some fun
in the sun!

beach party

monster party

sports party

fruit party

KV 19

7 Look at 6. Which party are they going to? When is it?

Cathy

James

Violet

Ben

8 Read the emails. Find the missing information (time, day of the week or address).

1

Inbox

Hi Jenny,

My birthday party is on Saturday.
Please bring your party CDs.
My address:
14 Stanley Street.
It's a green house.
Daniel, Sophie, Holly, Keira and Carl are coming.

See you on Saturday.
Ruby ☺

15:31

2

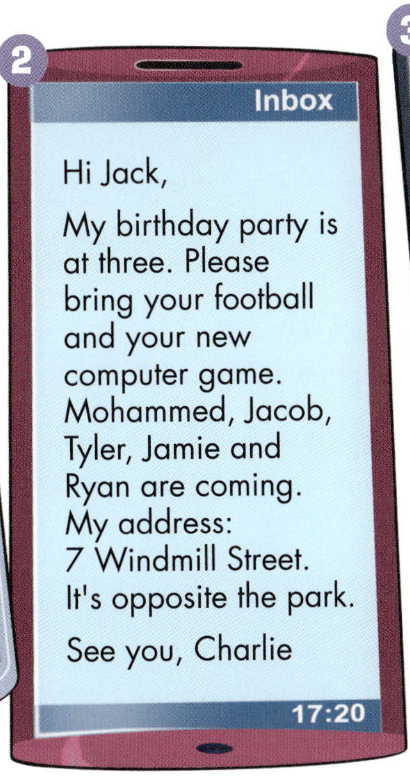

Inbox

Hi Jack,

My birthday party is at three. Please bring your football and your new computer game.
Mohammed, Jacob, Tyler, Jamie and Ryan are coming.
My address:
7 Windmill Street.
It's opposite the park.

See you, Charlie

17:20

3

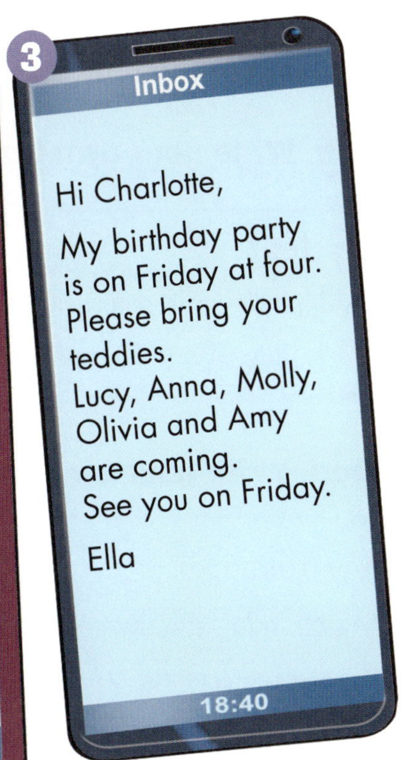

Inbox

Hi Charlotte,

My birthday party is on Friday at four.
Please bring your teddies.
Lucy, Anna, Molly, Olivia and Amy are coming.
See you on Friday.

Ella

18:40

☆ 9 Listen and read.

2 29

☆☆ 10 Change the dialogue and act it out.

My text

☆☆ 11 Read. Write your own text.

My text

My birthday's in summer.
It's in July. It's a Thursday this year.

☆☆☆ 12 Read. Write your own text.

My text

My birthday's in summer. It's in August. Then I have a big party.
I invite ten friends. We eat cake and sandwiches, and drink orange juice.
We play games and listen to music. We have lots of fun.

AB S. 31

Birthday presents

13 2 31 **Listen and point.**

ball

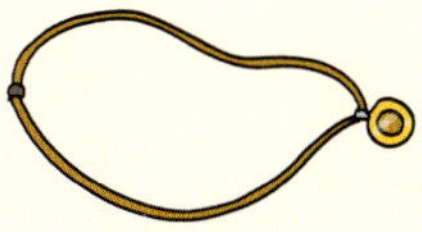
necklace

CD

car

ring

bike

T-shirt

book

pencil case

watch

skateboard

poster

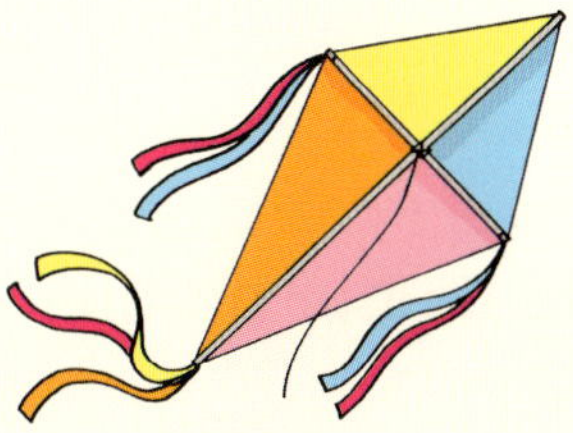
kite

trainers

coloured pencils

14 2 32 **Listen and read the poem.**

My birthday presents

A book, a ball, CDs, a car,
a birthday cake, a golden star.
A camera, a happy cow,
that's what's on my table now.

15 **Write your own poem.**

7 It's lunch time!

★ **1** **Work in pairs. How many words can you remember?**

We can remember … words.

★★ **2** **How many of the words can you read?**

carrots	tomatoes	potatoes	chicken	peppers	cake
pears	chips	cheese	cucumbers	apples	oranges

★ **3** 3 1 **Listen and point. Then test your partner.**

1. broccoli
2. egg
3. peas
4. rice
5. cheese sandwich
6. muesli bar
7. tomato soup
8. fish
9. yoghurt

★★ **4** **Play the memory game.**

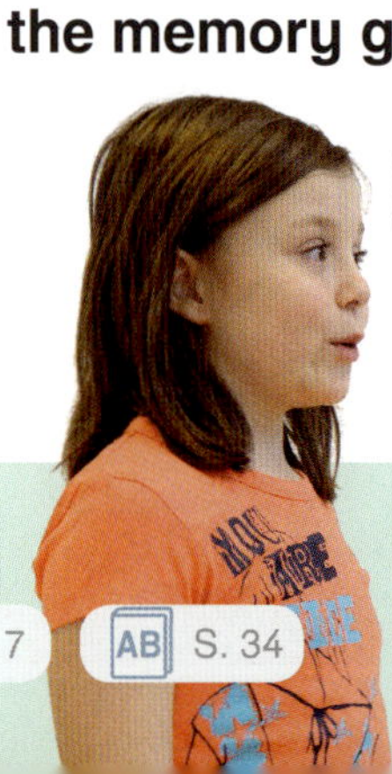

What's number three?

Right. Your turn.

I think it's *peas*.

 Poster 7 AB S. 34

★ 5 3–4 Listen. Sing the song.

Sweets

Well, here's a little story,
of a boy who loves his sweets.
But things go really wrong, so wrong.
Just listen to this song,
just listen to this song.

On Monday he has chocolate,
on Tuesday lollipops, oh yeah!
On Wednesday he has ice cream,
on Thursday lemon drops.
On Friday he has biscuits,
on Saturday a candy stick.
But on Sunday, oh, on Sunday,
on Sunday he feels sick!
Oh, no! Oh, no! Oh, no! …

Well, that's the little story,
of a boy who was so sick
that now he doesn't even eat
one tiny, tiny sweet!
Not a tiny, tiny sweet!

★★ 6 Look and read. Say.

Lucy

Dylan

Robert

Ella

1. There's a yoghurt, two carrots, an orange, a muesli bar and a cheese sandwich.
2. There's an egg, two carrots, an orange, a muesli bar and a cheese sandwich.
3. There's an egg, two carrots, an orange, a muesli bar and two cheese sandwiches.
4. There's a yoghurt, two apples, an orange, a muesli bar and a cheese sandwich.

LOOK!
a muesli bar
an orange

Lucy's lunch box is number …

7 It's lunch time!

★ 7 (CD 3, 7) **Listen and point. Then test your partner.**

1 milk
2 orange juice
3 mineral water
4 hot chocolate
5 tea

★★ 8 **Look and say.** (CD 3, 8) **Then listen and check.**

9 (CD 3/9) Listen and read.

Boy: Hello.

Woman: Hello. What can I get you?

Boy: I'm not very hungry today.
Just a tomato soup, please.
And I'm thirsty. Can I have a glass of water?

Woman: A tomato soup and a glass of water.
Here you are.

Boy: Thank you.

10 Change the dialogue in 9 and act it out.

11 (CD 3/10) Listen. Read and say *True* or *False*.

Girl: What have you got?

Boy: An apple and a cheese sandwich.

Girl: I've got a pear and two muesli bars.
Do you like muesli bars?

Boy: I love them.

Girl: OK, can I have your cheese sandwich?
You can have my muesli bars.

Boy: Great idea. Here you are.

Girl: Thanks. I'm so hungry.

Boy: So am I.

***True* or *False*?**

1. The girl likes cheese sandwiches.
2. The boy likes pears.
3. The girl gives him a pear.
4. The boy gives her a cheese sandwich.

12 Change the dialogue in 11 and act it out.

KV 23 AB S. 36

It's lunch time!

★ 13 Read the text. Find the correct picture.

He likes chicken. He doesn't like tomatoes. He likes orange juice.

1

2

3

4

It's …

★★ 14 Play a guessing game.

He likes … He doesn't like …

It's …

My text

★★ 15 Read. Write your own text.

My text

I like chicken. My favourite lunch is chicken and rice and a glass of orange juice. I don't like fish.

★★★ 16 Read. Write your own text.

My text

I like fish. My favourite lunch is fish and potatoes with a glass of mineral water. My number 2 favourite lunch is chicken with rice. I don't like broccoli. My mum loves chicken with rice. My dad often cooks it for her. In my favourite lunch box, there are two oranges, two muesli bars, a cheese sandwich and an egg.

AB S. 37

What's for lunch?

17 **Look at the photos. Guess the answers. Then watch the video and check.**

Which picture shows …
- a lunch box?
- a dinner lady?
- a school canteen?

Number 1 is …

A group project: What's for lunch?

Make drawings of food. Cut them out and make a lunch box.

Put in five things for your partner and give it to her / him.

Here's your lunch box.

Thank you. Ah, I've got …

★ 1 3 12 **Listen and point.**

1. It's quarter to three.
2. It's half past three.
3. It's quarter past seven.
4. It's six o'clock.
5. It's quarter past one.
6. It's five o'clock.
7. It's quarter to twelve.

★★ 2 **Ask a partner.**

LOOK!

It's **quarter past** four.

It's **half past** four.

It's **quarter to** five.

Going to a party

3 **Watch the story and say words you remember. Finish the sentences.**

4 14 **Listen and read.**

Anna: Come on, Jake. It's six o'clock.

Jake: Lots of time to finish the game.

…

Anna: Jake, it's half past six.
We're late!

Jake: Lots of time to finish the game.

Anna: OK, I'm going without you.

Jake: Wait, Anna, I'm coming!

5 **Do a role play.**

☆ 6 Listen. Say the rhyme.

3 15

Hickory …

Hickory dickory dock,
the mouse ran up the clock.
The clock struck one,
the mouse ran down.
Hickory dickory dock.

☆☆ 7 Read, look and say the names.

1. She gets up at seven o'clock. She goes to school at eight. She comes home at half past three. She meets her friends at four. She has dinner at half past six. She goes to bed at quarter to nine.

2. She gets up at seven o'clock. She goes to school at half past eight. She comes home at four o'clock. She meets her friends at quarter past four. She has dinner at seven. She goes to bed at nine o'clock.

Sally

Carmen

Midnight on the farm

★ **8** **Watch the story.** 3 16 **Listen and read.**

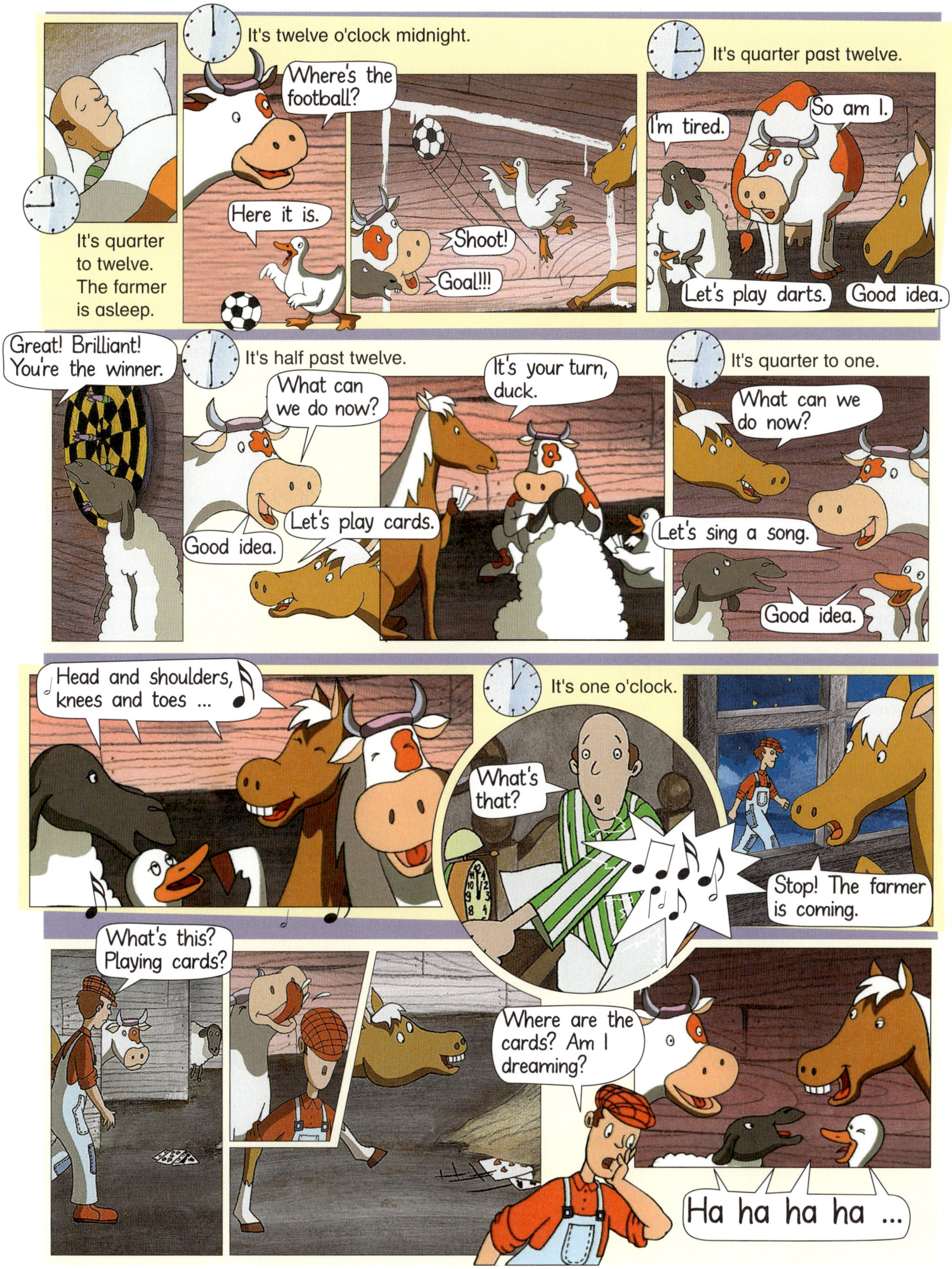

9 Listen and read.

I get up at seven. I have breakfast at quarter past seven. I go to school at ten to eight.
I come home at half past twelve.
I have lunch at twenty to one or at quarter to one.
I meet my friends at two.
I do my homework at five o'clock or ten past five.
We have dinner at seven.
I go to bed at quarter to nine.

10 Ask a partner.

My text

11 Read. Write your own text.

My text

I get up at seven o'clock.
I go to school at half past seven.
I come home at quarter past twelve.
I go to bed at nine.

12 Read. Write your own text.

My text

I get up at seven o'clock. I go to school at quarter to eight. School starts at ten to eight. I come home at twenty past twelve or half past twelve. I have lunch at one. In the afternoon I meet my friends, do my homework or play games with my brother. We have dinner at seven. Then I read or play computer games. I go to bed at half past eight.

 AB S. 41

Let's keep fit

13 **Test your partner. What can she/he do in a minute?**

1

2

3

4

Name	do sit-ups	bend your knees	jump	...
Nick	14	18	16	
Becky	10	15	12	

14 **How many times does your heart beat in a minute?**

sitting

after walking

after running

9 Body

☆ 1 Work in pairs. How many words can you remember?

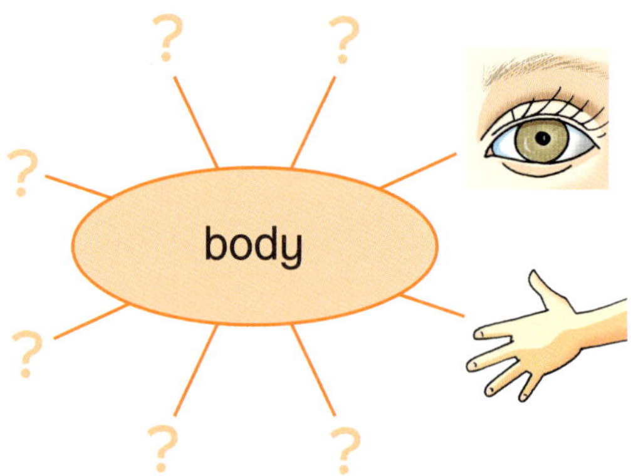

☆☆ 2 How many of the words can you read?

head	hand	arm	shoulder	eye
nose	mouth	ear	finger	knee
toe	leg	foot	tooth	

☆ 3 (CD 3, 19) Listen and point. Then test your partner.

1. a wide mouth
2. short black hair
3. long fair hair
4. a small nose
5. a big nose

☆☆ 4 Play the memory game.

Poster 9 | AB S. 42 | KV 27

5 3 21 **Look and listen. Speak.**

6 **Look, read and say.**

Her hair is ... .
Her nose is ... .
Her eyes are ... .
What's her name?

His hair is ... .
His nose is ... .
His eyes are ... .
What's his name?

His name is ... .
Her ...

7 3 23–24 **Listen. Sing the song.**

The body rock

Let's rock, the rock, the body rock, yeah!
Listen everybody,
get ready for the rock,
the rock, the rock, the body rock, yeah!

Shake your body to the beat,
arms and hands and legs and feet,
head and hair and ears and nose,
come on, shake, from head to toes.

Boys and girls, join in, please,
touch your toes and touch your knees,
touch your ears, your nose, your lips,
clap your hands and touch your hips.

8 Point and test your partner.

☆ 9 (3) 25–27 Listen. Do the chant.

Can you …?

Can you …
stand on your head,
snap your fingers,
wiggle your ears,
whistle a tune,
stand on one leg,
touch your toes
and wiggle your nose?

Of course I can!
I can stand on my head,
snap my fingers,
wiggle my ears,
whistle a tune,
stand on one leg,
touch my toes
and wiggle my nose!

☆ 10 Point and test your partner.

KV 28

The pirates

☆ **11** Watch the story. 3 28 Listen and read.

Monsters

12 Read, look and say.

His hair is blue, his nose is red and his teeth are yellow.
He has got four ears, three legs and two arms.

13 3 29 Listen to the poem and practise it.

His eyes are red.
His hair is pink.
His teeth are black.
He has got five legs
and four green arms.

Let's play a game.
What's his name?

14 Write your own poem and draw a picture.

Thanksgiving

☆ 1 3 30 **Listen and read.**

The fourth Thursday in November is Thanksgiving Day in the USA.
People say thank you for the harvest.
On Thanksgiving Day, families eat turkey, sweet potatoes and pumpkin pie.

☆ 2 **Look at the cartoon.**

The beginning of Thanksgiving

1620 in America:

The first winter:

The first spring:

The first Thanksgiving (autumn 1621):

Christmas

1 3 31 **Listen and read.**

Hi, I'm Christina from Cambridge. This is our Christmas.

December 24th: Christmas Eve

We hang up our Christmas stockings for the small presents. We put biscuits and a glass of milk for Father Christmas on a table.

December 25th: Christmas Day

We open our presents in the morning.

Later we have Christmas dinner. We eat turkey, Christmas pudding and mince pies. Here you can see my brother Pete, my grandma and grandpa, and my mum and dad.

We pull open Christmas crackers. In each cracker, there's a paper hat, a joke and small presents.

2 **Read. Say *England* or *Germany*.**

1. Children open their presents in the evening of December 24th.
2. Father Christmas gets biscuits and a glass of milk from the children.
3. Children open their presents on the morning of December 25th.
4. Children find the small presents in Christmas stockings.

Father Christmas is lost

★ **3** Watch the story. 3 32 Listen and read.

Easter

1 (CD 3, 33–35) Listen. Do the chant.

Here is an egg
and there's another,
One for me and one for my mother.
The bunny's feet go hop,
his ears go flop.
Hop, hop, hop,
flop, flop, flop.
Hop along, my little bunny.
You look very funny.
You look sweet,
oh, so sweet.

2 (CD 3, 36) Listen and read.

Before Easter, children make Easter cards at school. On Easter Sunday, many families have hot cross buns and boiled eggs for breakfast. For lunch, they have a big family meal. The children get big Easter eggs on Easter Sunday.

The bilby is a small Australian animal. It's in danger. Cats eat bilbies and rabbits eat their food. To help the bilby, Australians make chocolate Easter bilbies. 50 cents go to 'Save the bilby'.

3 Make a poster about your Easter. Speak.

Word list

English – German

A

act out	nachspielen
angry	wütend
animal	Tier
Art	Kunst
ask	fragen
attic	Dachboden
aunt	Tante
autumn	Herbst

B

back	zurück
backpack	Rucksack
bat	Fledermaus
beach	Strand
bear	Bär
the heart **beats**	das Herz **schlägt**
beautiful	(wunder)schön
bed	Bett
bee	Biene
behind	hinter
bend	beugen
big	groß
bird	Vogel
biscuits	Kekse
birthday	Geburtstag
board	Tafel
boat	Boot
body	Körper
book	Buch
boots	Stiefel
boy	Junge
breakfast	Frühstück
broccoli	Brokkoli
brother	Bruder
budgie	Wellensittich
buy	kaufen
Bye! / Bye-bye!	Tschüss!

C

cake	Kuchen, Torte
can / can't	können / nicht können
candle	Kerze
candy stick	Zuckerstange
canteen	(Schul-)Kantine
cap	Mütze, Kappe
careful	vorsichtig
carrot	Karotte
castle	Burg
chair	Stuhl
change	(ver)ändern
check	überprüfen
cheese (sandwich)	Käse(sandwich)
chicken	Huhn
child/children	Kind/Kinder
chips	Pommes frites
chocolate	Schokolade
Merry Christmas!	Frohe Weihnachten!
clap	klatschen
class/classroom	Klasse/Klassenzimmer
clever	klug
clock	(Wand)Uhr
close	schließen
clothes	Kleidung
cold	kalt
colour	Farbe; anmalen
come home	kommen, heimkommen
cook	kochen
crazy	verrückt
cupboard	Schrank
cut	schneiden

D

dad	Papa
dance	tanzen
dark	dunkel
daughter	Tochter
day	Tag
December	Dezember
desk	Tisch
dig	graben
dinner	Abendessen
dinner lady	Mitarbeiterin in der Schulkantine
do	tun, machen
draw	zeichnen
drink	trinken; Getränk
drum	trommeln
duck	Ente

E

ear	Ohr
Easter (bunny)	Ostern (Osterhase)
eat	essen
egg	Ei
every	jede/s
Excuse me.	Entschuldigung.

F

face	Gesicht
fair hair	helle Haare
false	falsch
family	Familie
famous	berühmt
Father Christmas	Weihnachtsmann
favourite (subject)	Lieblings(fach)
February	Februar
feel	fühlen
finish	beenden, abschließen
fish	Fisch
fit	fit; passen
flag	Flagge
fly	Fliege
flower	Blume
food	Speise
Friday	Freitag
friend	Freund/Freundin
friendly	freundlich
frog	Frosch
fruit	Frucht
fun / funny	Spaß / lustig

G

game	Spiel
German	Deutsch
get up	aufstehen
ghost	Geist
girl	Mädchen
give	geben
a **glass** of (milk)	ein **Glas** (Milch)
glue stick	Klebestift
go to bed	schlafen gehen
go to school	zur Schule gehen

goat	Ziege
goldfish	Goldfisch
good	gut
Good morning.	Guten Morgen.
grandma / grandpa	Großmutter / Großvater
great	großartig
guess	(er)raten
guest	Gast
guinea pig	Meerschweinchen
gym	Turnhalle

H

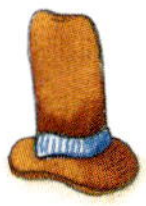

hair	Haare
It's **half past** one.	Es ist **halb** zwei.
happy	froh, glücklich
has (got) / have (got)	haben
hat	Hut
hate	hassen
haunted forest	verwunschener Wald
heart	Herz
help	helfen
Here you are.	(Hier), bitte sehr. / Da hast du es.
hips	Hüften
hole	Loch
homework	Hausübung
hoodie	Kapuzenpullover
hot	heiß
hot chocolate	heiße Schokolade
house	Haus
How are you?	Wie geht es dir / Ihnen / euch?
How many ...?	Wie viele ...?
hungry	hungrig
hurry up	sich beeilen

I

idea	Idee
inside	drinnen
introduce	(jemanden) **vorstellen**
invitation	Einladung

J

jacket	Jacke
January	Januar
July	Juli
jump	springen
June	Juni

K

king	König
kite	Drachen
knee	Knie
know	wissen

L

lake	See
late	spät
left	links; liegen gelassen
leg	Bein
lesson	Unterrichtsstunde
like / don't like	mögen / nicht mögen
lips	Lippen
listen	zuhören
little	klein
live	leben
lizard	Eidechse
log	Holzklotz

long	lang
look (for)	**schauen** (suchen)
love	lieben
lovely	nett, reizend
lunch / lunch box	Mittagessen / Pausenbrotdose

M

March	März
marry	heiraten
mat	Türmatte
Maths	Mathe(matik)
May	Mai
May I ...?	Darf ich bitte ...?
me	mir/mich
meat	Fleisch
meet	treffen
middle	Mitte
midnight	Mitternacht
(a glass of) **milk**	(ein Glas) **Milch**
mineral water	Mineralwasser
mittens	Fäustlinge
Monday	Montag
month	Monat
morning	Morgen
mouse/mice	Maus/Mäuse
mouth	Mund
muesli bar	Müsliriegel
mum	Mama
Music	Musik
musical	musikalisch

N

necklace	Halskette
next	nächste
nice	nett
Nice to meet you.	Freut mich, dich kennenzulernen.
night	Nacht
nobody	niemand
nose	Nase

O

It's one **o'clock**.	Es ist ein **Uhr**.
How **old** is it?	Wie **alt** ist es?
on	auf, am
open	öffnen
opposite	gegenüber
orange juice	Orangensaft
our	unser
outside	draußen
owl	Eule

P

PE	Turnen, Sport
pear	Birne
peas	Erbsen
pen	Stift, Füller
pencil / pencil case	Bleistift / Federmäppchen
pepper	Paprika
pet / pet shop	Haustier / Tierhandlung
picture	Bild
plane	Flugzeug
play	spielen
please	bitte
poem	Gedicht
potato(es)	Kartoffel(n)
practise	üben

Word list English – German

present	**Geschenk**
princess	**Prinzessin**
put on	**anziehen**

Q

quarter (past/to)	**Viertel** (nach/vor)
question	**Frage**

R

rabbit	**Hase**
rat	**Ratte**
read	**lesen**
remember	(sich) **erinnern**
rice	**Reis**
right	**rechts; richtig**
rubber	**Radiergummi**
ruler	**Lineal**
run	**laufen, rennen**

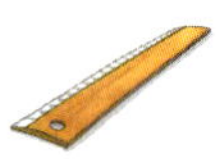

S

Saturday	**Samstag**
say	**sagen**
scared	**ängstlich, verängstigt**
scarf	**Schal**
scary shadow	**furchterregender Schatten**
school (things)	**Schule** (Schulsachen)
schoolbag	**Schultasche**
scissors	**Schere**
score a goal	ein Tor **schießen**
Scotland; Scottish	**Schottland; schottisch**
sea	**Meer**
seasons	**Jahreszeiten**
shake	**schütteln**
ship	**Schiff**
shirt	**Hemd**
shoes	**Schuhe**
short	**kurz**
shoulder	**Schulter**
I feel **sick.**	Mir ist **übel.**
silly	**albern**
sister	**Schwester**
skirt	**Rock**
sleep	**schlafen**
slippers	**Hausschuhe**
small	**klein**
snake	**Schlange**
socks	**Socken**
sofa	**Sofa**
something	**etwas**
Sorry. / I'm sorry.	**Entschuldigung.**
spider / spider's web	**Spinne / Spinnennetz**
spooky	**gruselig**
spring	**Frühling**
stamp	**stampfen**
star	**Stern**
stockings	**Strümpfe**
story/stories	**Geschichte/n**
strange	**merkwürdig**
stripe	**Streifen**
stupid	**dumm**
subject	**Schulfach**
summer	**Sommer**
Sunday	**Sonntag**
sure	**sicher, natürlich**
sweets	**Süßigkeiten**
swim	**schwimmen**

T

table	**Tisch**
take	**nehmen**
take off	**ausziehen**
(a cup of) **tea**	(eine Tasse) **Tee**
teacher	**Lehrer/in**
Thanks. / Thank you.	**Danke.**
Thanksgiving	**Erntedankfest**
think	**denken**
thirsty	**durstig**
thousands	**tausende**
tights	**Strumpfhose**
time	**Zeit**
tiny	**winzig**
tired	**müde**
It's ten **to** one.	Es ist zehn **vor** eins.
today	**heute**
toe(s)	**Zeh(en)**
tomato soup	**Tomatensuppe**
tomorrow	**morgen**
tooth/teeth	**Zahn/Zähne**
tortoise	**Schildkröte**
touch	**berühren**
trainers	**Turnschuhe**
trousers	**Hose**
truck	**Lastwagen**
true	**richtig, wahr**
try	**versuchen**
turkey	**Truthahn**

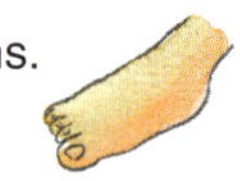

U

uncle	**Onkel**
under	**unter**

V

very	**sehr**

W

wait	**warten**
wake up	**aufwachen**
walk	**zu Fuß gehen**
want	**möchten**
wash	**waschen**
watch	**(Armband)Uhr; ansehen**
wear	**anhaben/tragen**
weekend	**Wochenende**
You're welcome.	**Gern geschehen.**
What?	**Was?**
When?	**Wann?**
Where?	**Wo?**
whistle	**pfeifen**
Who?	**Wer?**
Whose?	**Wessen?**
wide	**breit**
wiggle	**wackeln**
window	**Fenster**
with / without	**mit / ohne**
wood	**Wald**
woolly hat	**Wollmütze**
go **wrong**	**schiefgehen**

Y

year	**Jahr**
yoghurt	**Joghurt**